About Music In Action ...

Music In Action is a publisher of books for music educators, and, in particular, for band and choral directors.

Music In Action publications focus on both general and specific areas within the school choral and band fields.

At Music In Action, we strive to provide practical, readable, and affordable books for music educators at all levels.

CASE STUDY:

A SUCCESSFUL BAND PROGRAM

GORDON FUNG

with PATRICK DORIAN

Music in Action

P.O. Box 204   East Stroudsburg, PA 18301

Published by:

Music In Action
P.O. Box 204
East Stroudsburg, PA 18301

No portion of this book may be reproduced by any means, including photocopying, without written permission from the publisher.

ISBN 0-939139-04-9

Mr. Fung dedicates his writings in this book to his wife, Diane, and thanks her for her concern, appreciation and steadfast support.

To Mary: "For this time it isn't fascination, or a dream that will fade and fall apart. It's love this time, it's love my foolish heart."

To My Students: "Never be afraid to love, never be afraid to just be; Just cast away the chains of doubt, have the courage to be free. Open your eyes—you can fly."

-Pat Dorian

CONTENTS

1 INTRODUCTION

The East Stroudsburg Area School District is located in the Northeastern part of Pennsylvania that is referred to as the Poconos. This area, which includes the Delaware Water Gap, is a resort area with a limited amount of moderate sized industrial companies.

The borough of East Stroudsburg has a population of approximately 6,000 and is in Monroe county which has approximately 60,000 inhabitants.

This area is very accessible to Philadelphia (two hours and fifteen minute drive) and New York City (one hour and forty-five minute drive) which can afford our staff and students many cultural opportunities.

The 2,500 student school district encompasses a 214.3 square mile area which includes the borough of East Stroudsburg and the surrounding area of small villages. There are three elementary school buildings for grades Kindergarten through fifth, one building for all sixth grade students, one junior high school building for the seventh and eighth graders and one senior high school building for grades nine through twelve with an enrollment of 800 students.

The School District employs three instrumental music teachers. The elementary teacher works with students in grades four through six and gives lessons in the four buildings. The students are bussed once a week to one elementary school for a full band rehearsal. The junior high teacher works with the seventh and eighth graders, the junior high band, directs the jazz ensembles and assists the high school band director. Since there are no facilities for instrumental music in the junior high school, all instruction and rehearsals for the junior high students are done next door in the high school bandroom. The high school teacher works with students in grades nine through twelve, directing the Marching-Show Band and the Concert Band.

These three teachers work with a total of 325 students in the Elementary (115 students), Junior High (85 students) and Senior High (125 students) schools. Additional support is supplied by the school district with the employment of a part-time secretary (20 hours a week) in the high school band office, a band front advisor for the high school Marching-Show Band and a majorette advisor for an intramural program for girls in grades three through eight.

The band program was begun in 1934 and over the years has been very proud of its tradition of quality education. Clement Wiedinmyer started the program and continued teaching in East Stroudsburg until his retirement in 1968. He was joined by Robert Zellner in 1956 who directed the high school band from 1960-1968 and then John Casagrande who was the director from 1968 to 1978. The present director is Gordon Fung and his associate Patrick Dorian.

Over the years, the various bands have been recognized for their excellence by winning a state-wide competition ten times (1940-1957), high ratings at music festivals, parade performances such as Pennsylvania Governor's Inauguration Parade (1967), King Orange Jamboree Parade in Miami (1976), Miss America Pageant Parade (1981), the Canadian Thanksgiving Day Parade in Ontario, Canada (1982 and 1983), performances at the state music convention, numerous performances for National Football League and Canadian Football League games, eleven consecutive "Superior" ratings at the Pennsylvania Music Educators Association Adjudication Festivals (1974-1985) and most recently a jazz program that has been recognized at the Berklee and University of New Hampshire Jazz Festivals (1984 and 1985).

In recognition of this tradition, the school held a Dedication Concert for the auditorium to be named the Clement Wiedinmyer Auditorium. The Elementary, Junior High and Senior High Concert Bands all performed, and each premiered a composition by composer Elliot Del Borgo commissioned for the occasion. It was interesting to note that the concert (March 5, 1985) was attended by several members of the original 1934 band who still live in the community.

The present structure of the program can be considered a direct result of this tradition of excellence through the hard work of the first three directors.

2   THE MARCHING-SHOW BAND

The Marching-Show Band performs primarily during the months of September, October and November and the only additional activities are the local Saint Patrick's Day Parade in March and the Memorial Day Parade in May. In order to have a satisfying and efficient three months of performances, a great deal of preparation is done by the director, his associate and the band prior to the first performance in September.

Music

The initial project is to select and order the music for the marching season. This is done by the directors in May and June by listening to the many demonstration records and tapes that are received free of charge from the various publishers of marching band music. The consideration for selection of music is based upon the need for variety of musical styles within the format of the half time show.

The format has included: 1) an up tempo "opener," 2) a Latin/jazz tune, 3) a combination of a student-composed drum solo that leads directly into a band tune and incorporates the same rhythmic feel, 4) a relaxed lyrical tune and 5) a "closer" that ends with a loud tutti section. The need for songs 2, 3, and 4 has been flexible depending upon the drill design, the amount of instructional time available, need for band front routines and the overall timing of the show.

The selection of each song is based in order of priorities upon: 1) the harmonic structure, 2) the rhythmic "feel" and tempo, 3) melodic line, 4) scoring and 5) the time requirements of a 10-12 minute half time show. Once the selection of arrangements has been made, the music is ordered prior to the end of school in June. The music is catalogued, filed and then distributed to the next year's band members before the summer vacation.

During the marching season, the band will do three different half time shows and this requires the selection of fifteen songs. The initial show is used for the first two home games, cavalcades, a professional football game and several away games. The second show will be incorporated into the school's Homecoming activities and the final show is developed by the senior members of the band and performed for the last two football games.

Also, every other year a half time show is presented by the entire music department with the Elementary Band playing a song, the Junior High Band playing a song, the Marching-Show Band playing a song and then the three bands combining together in one large formation and playing a song such as "I'd Like to Teach the World to Sing," "It's a Small World," or a simplified arrangement of a Sousa march.

Band Front

Another aspect of the marching band that is taken care of prior to the end of the school year is the band front. The band front consists of the majorette, rifle and silk squads. Any interested student is required to attend five instructional practices during April and May and then participate in a tryout. A captain of each squad and the drum major are also selected at this time. See Figures 1 through 4 for the tryout requirements.

The tryout is judged by the band director, associate director and three or four "outsiders." The band front advisor is not included as a judge in an effort to eliminate any sense of partiality since she will be working with the three squads the coming year.

Once the selection is made, the captains and the new members of the band front are encouraged to attend one of the many summer band front camps available to high school students. Quite often they will hold car washes or bake sales to help defray the expenses for the camp. The camps that the girls have attended are generally a five-day session, cost approximately $150 and are located within a 70-mile radius of East Stroudsburg.

Instrumentation

The instrumentation of the Marching-Show Band is divided into the three basic areas of brass, woodwind and percussion. The brasses include trumpets, trombones, mellophoniums and sousaphones with the latter three instruments being supplied by the school. The school supplies a King 4B trombone, which is a relatively large bore instrument, for each student. The trombones are furnished for the students because of the nature of the marching band. With so much movement (and occasional confusion when learning a new show) and the slide protruding so much, the instrument can quite easily be dented. Mellophoniums are furnished for the French hornists, since the bell front instrument projects its sound

EAST STROUDSBURG HIGH SCHOOL MARCHING-SHOW BAND RIFLE SQUAD TRYOUTS

1. COMMANDS (10)

2. HAND SPINS
    LEFT (10)
    RIGHT (10)

3. FLIP FLOP
    LEFT (10)
    RIGHT (10)

4. BUTTERFLIES (15)

5. AERIALS
    LEFT (20)
    RIGHT (20)

6. MARCH ROUTINE (20)

7. TWIRL ROUTINE (20)

Figure 1

EAST STROUDSBURG HIGH SCHOOL
MARCHING-SHOW BAND
DRUM MAJOR TRYOUTS

1. ROUTINE
   CREATIVITY (10)
   EXECUTION (15)
   1 WORD COMMENT

2. CONDUCTING
   STYLE (10)
   CLARITY (10)

3. ALMA MATER
   PITCH (10)
   CONDUCTING (10)

4. VERBAL COMMANDS
   VOICE (10)
   AUTHORITY (10)

5. SOLO ROUTINE
   CREATIVITY (10)
   EXECUTION (15)
   1 WORD COMMENT

6. ON THE SPOT MACE (20)

7. ON THE SPOT CONDUCTING (20)

8. TEMPOS

	Tempo	Rhythm
160	(5)	(5)
112	(5)	(5)
96	(5)	(5)
82	(5)	(5)

Figure 2

EAST STROUDSBURG HIGH SCHOOL
MARCHING-SHOW BAND
MAJORETTE SQUAD TRYOUTS

1. STANDING TWIRLS
   THUMB FLIP (10)
   FINGER TWIRL (10)
   FLARE SEQUENCE (10)
   DOUBLE TURN (10)
   HALF TURN (10)

2. MARCHING TWIRLS
   AIRPLANE SEQUENCE (10)
   FLAT SPIN SEQUENCE (10)
   FLARE SEQUENCE (10)
   3/4 TURN TOSS (10)

3. DANCE ROUTINE (20)

4. TWIRL ROUTINE (20)

5. MARCH ROUTINE (20)

6. COMMANDS (10)

Figure 3

EAST STROUDSBURG HIGH SCHOOL MARCHING-SHOW BAND SILK SQUAD TRYOUTS

1. COMMANDS (10)

2. PUSH PULLS (10)

3. SLANTS (10)

4. SPINS (10)
 FRONT (15)
 SIDE (15)

5. BUTTERFLIES (10)

6. MARCH ROUTINE (20)

7. TWIRL ROUTINE (20)

Figure 4

forward toward the audience. A brass sousaphone is furnished for the tubists. Although the metal instruments are much heavier than their fiberglass counterparts, they have a much better projection of sound.

The woodwinds include piccolos, Bb soprano clarinets, alto saxophones and tenor saxophones. The school supplies piccolos for all the flutists (16). The piccolo sound carries much better than the flute and thus compliments the woodwind sound and also enforces the trumpet line since in most stock arrangements, they play the same part. The director encourages clarinetists to play alto or tenor saxophone in the marching band. As with the piccolo versus the flute, the saxophone sound carries more than the clarinet sound. All tenor saxophones are furnished for the students and for the clarinetist who plays alto saxophone an instrument is also supplied.

A great deal of emphasis in the percussion section is placed upon the four "pitched" bass drums. Although extra rehearsal time is required to develop the four players on the "pitched" bass drums, they will create the rhythmic feel for the entire band. Also, they will often be rehearsed with the sousaphones to solidify the rhythmic and harmonic structure of the marching band arrangements. The additional percussion instruments are the snare drums, one or two sets of tri-toms and cymbals. Quite often, the double reed players from the Concert Band will play either cymbals or bass drum.

Marching Band Camp

In preparation for the Fall performances, the band rents a camp located approximately 40 miles from East Stroudsburg. The necessary facilities at the camp must include: 1) dining hall and kitchen staff to accommodate 130 people, 2) cabins to house the boys and girls in separate areas, 3) a lined football field, 4) gymnasium for the band front to work in case of inclement weather, 5) a lighted area (such as tennis courts) for the band front to work after sunset and 6) a swimming pool or lake.

The camp staff includes the director and associate director, a percussion instructor, the band front advisor, a nurse and two or three chaperones. The director is responsible for woodwind sectionals and the full band rehearsals, the associate director works with the brass section, the percussion instructor rehearses the percussionists, the band front advisor is responsible for coordinating the majorette, rifle and silks squads, the nurse is responsible for all medication and the chaperones are in charge of bed checks, cabin inspections and chaperoning during free time. Since there is very little "free" time for the students, there is not a great deal of "work" for the chaperones.

The day is divided into an equal amount of sectional rehearsals and full band rehearsals. See Figure 5 for a complete schedule. During the first two days of the brass and woodwind sectionals, the fundamentals of tone production are emphasized with very little attention given to the music that is to be performed. During the first two days the band front will work on basic skills while the captains will take time to develop the routines for the initial show. The percussion section will also work on basic skills while using an amplified metronome to develop an accurate rhythmic pulse.

During these first two days at camp the full rehearsals on the field are spent developing a physical and mental discipline using basic left-face, right-face, parade rest, attention and marching eight steps to five yards. After the physical coordination and concentration is

EAST STROUDSBURG HIGH SCHOOL
MARCHING-SHOW BAND

MONDAY		TUESDAY		WEDNESDAY	
9:00	REPORT	6:15	RISE	6:15	RISE
9:45	DEPART	7:00	BREAKFAST	7:00	BREAKFAST
10:45	ARRIVE CAMP	8:00	SECTIONALS	8:00	SECTIONALS
12:00	LUNCH	9:30	FIELD	9:30	FIELD
1:00	FIELD WITH EQUIPMENT	11:30	LUNCH	11:30	LUNCH
3:30	SECTIONALS	12:45	SECTIONALS	12:45	SECTIONALS
5:00	DINNER	2:15	FIELD	2:15	FIELD
6:15	SECTIONALS	4:30	DINNER	4:30	DINNER
7:15	FIELD WITH EQUIPMENT	6:15	SECTIONALS	6:15	FIELD
8:30	MUSIC	7:15	FIELD	8:30	MUSIC
9:45	BREAK	8:30	MUSIC	9:45	BREAK
10:15	IN CABINS	9:45	BREAK	10:00	PIZZA & SODA
10:45	LIGHTS OUT	10:15	CABINS	10:40	CABINS
		10:45	LIGHTS OUT	11:15	LIGHTS OUT

Figure 5

BAND CAMP SCHEDULE

THURSDAY		**FRIDAY**	
6:15	RISE	6:15	RISE
7:00	BREAKFAST	7:00	BREAKFAST
8:00	SECTIONALS	8:00	SECTIONALS
9:30	FIELD	9:00	FIELD
11:30	LUNCH	11:30	LUNCH
12:45	SECTIONALS	1:00	FIELD
1:00	FIELD	2:00	LOAD BUS
4:30	DINNER	3:30	RETURN
6:15	FIELD		
8:30	BREAK		
9:30	HOT DOGS AND SODA		

developed to the point of 90 seconds of "facing" movements without a mistake, the band will then march the field playing the B-flat major scale with each scale tone being held for five yards.

The next two and a half days are used to teach the show. The music and the routines are rehearsed in sectionals and the drill is taught on the field in 32 count segments.

The drill is designed and charted by the director. The preparation time by the director is quite demanding, requiring about seven hours to design and chart just one minute of a show. The charts are given to the student section leaders (generally two per section) who set the line up of their section. It is important to carefully explain each chart to the section leaders so they clearly understand what their section must do. This careful preparation results in an efficient use of rehearsal time and develops a respect by the sections for their leader.

This establishment of student leadership is one of the primary functions of the five day camp. By the third day a good portion of sectional time is run by the section leaders with the directors assisting the students but much of the actual teaching being done by section leaders. By the fifth day the entire show has been taught and there is a sense of accomplishment and finality.

However, the students are reminded that the last day of camp is actually the beginning of the school year. They are also reminded that through hard work, co-operation and student leadership, a great deal was accomplished and if this system is continued, the band will function very well throughout the school year.

The cost of the camp is financed by a $3,400.00 donation from the Band Parents organization and the cost per student is approximately $55.00. This covers the expenses for the four nights and five days, all meals, staff and clinican fees and the incidentals for hot dogs, pizza, soda and watermelon.

Rehearsal Format

During the school year the band does all its rehearsing during the regularly scheduled band period. The only consistent exceptions to this rehearsal schedule are the three band front squads. They are scheduled for a two-hour rehearsal once a week after school. Since all of their routines are taught by rote, as opposed to the instrumentalists who have printed music to learn, it is necessary for them to have additional practice time.

Since the instruction and rehearsing is done within the confines of the school day, it is imperative that the time is used very efficiently. All rehearsing is done outdoors (except during inclement weather) on a practice field next to the high school. The rehearsal format includes: 1) sectional warm-ups, 2) music rehearsal by the full band, 3) teaching new drill work and/or rehearsing drills that have been taught and 4) final announcements about an upcoming performance, trip, fund-raiser, etc.

At the beginning of the season a good portion of the rehearsal is used for fundamentals but as the season progresses more time is needed to teach a new show with the fundamentals of marching being fairly well established. Using the same system as at camp, the fundamental drills start with facing movements until the full band goes 90 seconds without a mistake. Then the band marches from end zone to end zone to develop the eight steps to five yards while playing a scale. Since the band incorporates both a high step which was popular in the Big Ten college bands and also the low step which is used by today's drum corps, a good deal of time is spent on both styles.

At the beginning of the season the third portion of the rehearsal is used to practice problem spots in the show learned at camp. As the season progresses, this part of the rehearsal is used to learn a new show.

The final five minutes are set aside for announcements, a compliment or a necessary word of criticism to keep the band headed in a positive direction. The announcements are made at the end of rehearsal so they are fresh in the students' minds when they leave the band room. It also gives them a few minutes to relax before going on to their next class.

Performances

The Marching-Show Band performances during the school year include: 1) high school football games, 2) two cavalcades/adjudications, 3) parades, 4) a Sit Down Revue at the end of the football season, 5) a professional football game and 6) unique "fund raisers."

The school's football team plays eleven games with five home games one year and then six home games the next year. The schedule starts with Labor Day Weekend and concludes on Thanksgiving Day. When five home games are scheduled, the show that is learned at camp is performed at the first two games, the third game is used for the Homecoming festivities and then the seniors write a show that is performed at the last two home games.

The same type of format is used when there are six home games except that the third game is used for a show that presents the elementary and junior high bands with the high school band, then followed by the Homecoming and senior show. This show has each of the three bands play a song by themselves and then they combine to make one large formation and play a selection such as "It's A Small World" and the "Alma Mater."

For two of the away games a pep band is used instead of taking the full band. The Pep Band is on a volunteer basis but approximately 85 students sign up to play in the Pep Band. The Pep Band usually plays at the game farthest from East Stroudsburg and the final away game of the season.

The cavalcade/adjudications are hosted by neighboring schools. At the Cavalcade, each band performs its show giving the participating bands an opportunity to see what music and drill work is being used by other bands. The Adjudication is hosted by another local high school and each participating band is evaluated by a panel of five judges and awarded a rating but not a ranking. The bands receive a printed score sheet and a cassette recording of comments from each judge. These comments have proved to be most valuable to the band for future performances.

The band participates in the community's parades which include Halloween, Veteran's Day, Saint Patrick's Day and Memorial Day. The music selected is appropriate for the occasion. A traditional march or patriotic song is used for Veteran's Day and Memorial Day and the "Notre Dame Fight Song" is used for the Saint Patrick's Day Parade. The Halloween Parade is a special event for the band with everyone coming in costume. Although there are no requirements, most sections select a group theme for their costume. For example, one year the sousaphones dressed as ghosts, the seven saxophones as The Seven Dwarfs, the trombones came dressed for a toga party and the percussionists actually rode on an old ambulance and wore medical attire.

The Sit Down Revue is presented in the gymnasium on the Friday prior to the Thanksgiving Day football game. The music and band front routines from the fall season are performed at the Revue and also four or five selections are played by the junior high band. The high school band will play approximately twenty marching band tunes with the conducting being shared by the drum major, the director and associate director. Each of the band front squads is featured in two routines and then they combine for the final selection, "God Bless America." The Revue is also a fund raiser as tickets are sold and the band Parents organization has a bake sale in the lobby.

Each year, the band combines a fall trip with a performance for a professional football team. Performances have been for the Washington Redskins, New York Giants, New England Patriots, Philadelphia Eagles, Buffalo Bills, Hamilton (Ontario) Tiger Cats, Toronto Argonauts and the Ottowa Rough Riders. In all cases, the management, security and public relations personnel have been most cooperative and courteous to the band members and the staff.

In order to receive an invitation to perform at a professional game, correspondence is initiated by the director in February for an October performance. The correspondence includes a cover letter, photograph of the band, resume of the band's accomplishments and cassette recordings of the marching and concert bands.

Once a date and fee (ranges from $1,000 to $2,000) have been agreed upon, the director will: 1) write to the city's chamber of commerce requesting sightseeing information, possibility of an additional performance and a listing of hotels/motels in the area that are preferably near the stadium and, 2) arrange for chartered buses. The two primary concerns are the cost and quality of the lodging and meals. Selection of lodging is based upon cost per room (four students to a room), a large enough facility in order to separate boys and girls rooms by floors or separate wings of the building and if possible, a dining room large enough to handle 140-150 people. It has been the objective of the director to have some of the meals on the trip as sit down meals. However, this can be most difficult because of cost and also it can take a long time to serve this number of people. Quite often a buffet type dinner or breakfast is a satisfactory alternative.

The financing of the trip is covered by the fee from the football team, a $2,500-$3,500 donation from the Band Parents organization and the balance is covered by the individual student. The average trip will provide transportation, two nights in a quality hotel/motel, breakfasts and dinners and sight-seeing admissions with the individual's cost being approximately $70-$80.

Since the school district is located in a resort area, the band has been called upon to perform for some unique situations and in turn contributions are made to the band. Some of the performances have included a "surprise" birthday party appearance by the band in full uniform playing Happy Birthday, marching through a convention for a sales representative's Fall Kick-off meeting, July 4th parade and a "surprise" appearance at a "Roasting" party for the head salesmen at another convention. In addition to the general donation, each participating student will receive either refreshments or a complimentary visit to a local fast food establishment.

3 CONCERT BAND

The Concert Band functions from December to June. The primary activities for Concert Band members include an audition, Concert Band Camp, Instrumental Music Department Concert, hosting a Pennsylvania Music Educators Association's Concert Band Adjudication Festival, the P.M.E.A. District, Regional and All-State Band and Orchestra Festivals and the Spring Concert.

Scheduling

The students receive their instruction during the daily band rehearsal period and a weekly group lesson. The high school schedule has three half hour lunch periods. The band members eat during the first lunch period, have homeroom and then rehearse during the second two lunch periods. There are many advantages to this schedule.

Homeroom is held in the auditorium to accomodate the 120 students in the band. During this time the daily attendance is recorded by having the students sit in alphabetical order by grades and the daily announcements are read. Also during this time announcements pertaining to band activities are made. There is an additional advantage to having a "band" homeroom since the band director makes announcements about club meetings, scholarships available to members of the senior class, and in general becomes aware of the other activities that band students participate in. Report cards are also distributed in homeroom. This gives the director an opportunity to encourage students who need help and give praise to the students who have earned good grades.

There are several advantages to the scheduling of the band period during the lunch schedule: 1) the rehearsal time is one hour instead of the regular 42 minute period; 2) the period is never eliminated due to an assembly program, pep rally or even early dismissal for inclement weather; due to the five hours per week rehearsal time (and also efficient use of that time) the band hardly ever rehearses after school (even for the marching band).

Rehearsal Format

The daily rehearsal is divided into three segments: 1) warm-up for the entire band, 2) rehearsal, 3) small ensemble performance.

The wind players warm up with The Caruso exercises. Incidentally, The Caruso warm-up exercises are also used by the Marching-Show Band.

Additional exercises done on a rotating rather than daily basis include a tonguing exercise, an exercise to control volume and one for balance, blend and intonation.

After the warm-up period, approximately 30 minutes are used to rehearse the music that is to be performed. During this time, an effort is made to keep the students playing as much as possible but, of course, there are always specific needs for an individual section. The most efficient way to correct problems is to play the passage slowly and accurately until it is comfortable.

The last ten minutes of the rehearsal are reserved for ensemble performances. Each member of the band is required to play in a small (two to six player) ensemble. The students may play with whatever combination of instruments they like and in some cases will transpose a part in order for a flutist to play a duet with her best friend, an alto clarinetist. The emphasis on this ensemble program is to develop an appreciation and respect for each member of the band regardless of an individual's ability. The only requirements are 1) that each band member must perform; 2) that they may rehearse the entire band period on the day of their performance; and 3) that there be only one person on a part. This ensemble program has been very successful and has even been an outlet for student compositions. This program is possible because the band has developed an extensive library of solo, duet and ensemble music from which the students can choose.

Rotating Lesson

Each student is scheduled for a weekly homogeneous group lesson. The number of students in a lesson is determined by the instrumentation of the band and the needs of each individual band member. The groups range from three oboists to possibly 12 flutists. In theory, each student is excused from class on a rotating schedule to attend a lesson once a week unless a test or quiz is given during the scheduled lesson period. When the student has a test, he is to make up the lesson during the same period on Friday. However, the attendance at lessons is very flexible since many of the band members are in "honors" classes and feel many pressures (real or imagined) to attend their academic subjects. Therefore, the director will frequently work with students after school or during a student's study hall to make up the lesson time. This instructional time is very important since only 10% of the students study privately.

During the lesson, very few instruction books are used. Instead, scale sheets have been reproduced for each specific instrument that covers the range of the instrument and a set of 40 rhythmic exercises have been developed for each band member to learn. In addition to the scales and reading rhythms, time can be taken to deal with specific problems of an instrument such as hand position in the French horn bell, legato tonguing on a trombone, vibrato, etc. As performances draw near, a good portion of the lesson time is spent on band music.

Audition

Each member of the band is auditioned in January during a lesson period. The audition, done individually by the director, is used to establish the seating of the band and to determine that a student has achieved at least the minimum level of skill to comfortably participate in performances with the band.

The auditon consists of 1) the chromatic scale (slurred) for the full range of the instrument; 2) the major scales (tongued) for the range of the instrument; 3) a designated solo; and 4) two sight-reading excerpts. The solo is the same solo as required for the Pennsylvania Music Educators Association District Band audition. This is done to encourage students to audition for District Band and yet does not require extra preparation for the student. See Figure 6.

If a student does not "pass" the initial audition, he is then re-auditioned but required to play only the chromatic

AUDITION FORM
EAST STROUDSBURG HIGH SCHOOL

NAME____DATE_____________

INSTRUMENT_____________________________________

SCALES:

Chromatic (slurred) (15)　　　　　　　___________

Major (tongued) (5 each)　　　　　　___________

C　　D♭　　D　　E♭　　F　　G♭　　G　　A♭　　A　　B♭　　B

SOLO:

Tone (25)　　　　　　　　　___________

Articulation (15)　　　　　　___________

Rhythm (20)　　　　　　　___________

Technique (20)　　　　　　___________

Phrasing (20)　　　　　　　___________

Foot Tapping (15)　　　　　___________

SIGHT-READING:

10 points each　　　　　　　___________

TOTAL _______________

Figure 6

and major scales. He is given as much time as necessary to learn the scales but is not allowed to play in performances until "passing" this second audition.

Seating/Challenge

After the week long auditioning process is completed, the scores are tallied and the ranking of the students is posted. The next process is the seating of the band. The top ranking players are placed throughout each section in an effort to eliminate having all the stronger players on the first part and all the weaker players on the third or fourth part. For example, the clarinet players who ranked 1, 2 and 3 are placed on the first part; players 4, 5 and 6 are placed on the second part and players 7, 8 and 9 are placed on the third part. To give a feeling of importance to these students, they receive an asterisk by their name on any printed program as a Principal Player. The remaining students are seated the same way with players 10 and 11 on the first part; players 12, 13 and 14 on the second part and players 15, 16, 17 and 18 on third part.

If a student is disappointed with this ranking he may challenge the student above him. The challenge, which is heard individually by the director, consists of the chromatic and major scales, the band music of the student being challenged, and sight reading.

Concert Band Camp

At the end of January, the Concert Band goes to "Camp." The band leaves after school on Friday and returns late Saturday evening. The camp is held about an hour's drive away with the housing done at a motel and all rehearsals and meals at a nearby college. This is generally a good time to use college facilities since many colleges are on break during the month of January.

The staff taken to the camp includes the three instru-mental music teachers, a percussion instructor, a nurse and/or doctor and three or four women chaperones. There is generally a need for more women chaperones since the female population of the band outnumbers the male popula-tion almost two to one.

Upon arrival the band members first check-in to their motel rooms. Then they go to the college, unload all the equipment into the rehearsal facility and have dinner in the dining hall.

After dinner, a full rehearsal is followed by brass, woodwind and percussion sectionals. During the rehearsals the emphasis is based upon the students listening to each other to develop their fundamental skills of tuning and balanced ensemble playing. In the sectionals a good portion of time is used for instructional purposes such as double tonguing for the brass players, the proper handling of the accessory percussion equipment, tonguing on a single reed instrument, emphasising the importance of a "good" reed, etc. The remainder of the rehearsal schedule on Friday is a full rehearsal with three or four pieces handed out by the librarians for sight-reading. The con-clusion of the evening is pizza and soda for the students in the college dining hall.

On Saturday, the morning schedule is similar to Fri-day evening. However, in the afternoon there is a full rehear-sal for more sight reading and then sectionals for specific instruments plus woodwind and brass quintets. In the sec-tionals, the students are given one to two hours to rehearse and "polish" a piece that they will then perform for the band. It is the responsibility of the first chair players to bring the necessary music to camp and to lead the rehearsal. See Figure 7 for a complete band camp schedule.

EAST STROUDSBURG HIGH SCHOOL
CONCERT BAND CAMP
JANUARY 24-JANUARY 25, 1986
LAFAYETTE COLLEGE

FRIDAY

6:00 P.M.	Arrive and unload
6:30 P.M.	Dinner
7:30 P.M.	Full rehearsal on stage
8:45 P.M.	1. Percussion on stage
	2. Brasses = 40
	3. Woodwinds = 60
9:30 P.M.	Full rehearsal on stage
10:00 P.M.	Pizza

SATURDAY

8:00 A.M.	Breakfast
8:45 A.M.	Full rehearsal on stage, percussion bandroom
9:45 A.M.	Woodwinds-60, brass-40, percussion
11:00 A.M.	Lunch
1:45 P.M.	Full rehearsal on stage with percussion
3:30 P.M.	Flute-18, clarinet-17, oboe-3, bassoon-2, alto clarinet-4, bass clarinet-4, sax-12, trumpet-17, horn-8, trombone and euphonium-9, tuba-4, percussion on stage
4:30 P.M.	Full rehearsal on stage
6:00 P.M.	Dinner
7:00 P.M.	Full rehearsal on stage
7:30 P.M.	Pack up
9:30 P.M.	Return home

Figure 7

Music Check-Off/Sectionals

As a performance approaches, it is the responsibility of each band member to satisfactorily play all his music for either the director or his section leader. To keep a record of each student, a large chart is posted on the bulletin board with the band members listed by sections and a column for each piece next to his name.

The chart serves several purposes: 1) an emphasis that everyone is expected to learn the music; 2) the "goal-oriented" student is very anxious to see all his music checked off; 3) the chart creates a great deal of interest and peer pressure on the students to get their music checked off; and 4) a great deal of instruction is given each student by either the section leader or the director.

The use of the chart is most effective for the "goal-oriented" student and it also creates interest in what individual or what section is first in learning the music. Prior to the beginning of the school day, students will stop by the bandroom to "study" the chart and quite often a section will have an extra rehearsal in order to get its music checked off.

Sectionals are held at the discretion of the section leader and the only two stipulations from the director are that the sectional be at least an hour long and that all members of the section be present. Because of work schedules or athletic team practices, the sectionals may occur at rather odd times. It is not unusual for a section to rehearse at 7:30 P.M. or 6:30 A.M. prior to the start of the school day at 7:52 A.M. The early hour sectionals necessitate the director opening the bandroom for the students and then he goes to an all-night supermarket to buy doughnuts for the students. They certainly deserve something extra for their dedication. In fact, some sections enjoy the unique situation of meeting at McDonalds at

6:00 A.M. for breakfast and then having their sectional afterwards.

Department Concert

The dress for all Concert Band performances is the traditional concert attire of formal black. The boys wear tuxedos and the girls wear a floor length black dress or skirt and blouse. The tuxedos are owned by the band but the girls are responsible for their concert attire.

The first concert of the year is on a school night in March and is presented by the Elementary, Junior High and Senior High Concert Bands. Each band prepares three or four selections in an effort to keep the program as short as possible. This concert gives the audience and the students an opportunity to see the progress of the student abilities from the youngest to the oldest students. It also gives each band an opportunity to get a concert situtation experience but eliminates the pressure of preparing a great deal of music.

This concert has also been used for a special occasion. When the auditorium was posthumously renamed Clement Wiedinmyer Auditorium in honor of the band's first director, the program was a unique Dedication Concert. Composer Elliot Del Borgo was commissioned to compose a piece for each band.

In an effort to have each piece compatible with the ensemble that would give the premiere performance, Dr. Del Borgo requested a list of instrumentation and a recording of each band. In addition to the difficulty of the piece and instrumentation restrictions, two other important considerations were to have the score and parts prepared professionally (this saves a lot of rehearsal time) and to receive the score and parts in time for adequate preparation prior to the concert. With all of these considerations of a practical nature being met, the concert became a very special event since Dr. Del Borgo was present to rehearse and conduct his music.

Adjudication Festival

Each Spring the band hosts and participates in a Pennsylvania Music Educators Association sponsored Adjudication Festival. The objective of the Adjudication Festival is to provide a program in which elementary, middle school/junior high and senior high bands may participate regardless of school size or proficiency of the band. By selecting a grade level of music as determined in the National Band Association's "Selected Music List," the band is able to perform music best suited for its abilities. Each band receives a cassette tape of its performance with the judges comments on it, a score sheet from each of the judges, and a participation plaque.

The format for the Festival includes a concert performance of two of the three prepared selections. The judges choose one selection to be performed and the director chooses the other piece. The sight reading material used is one grade level lower than the grade level of the band's concert performance. The band receives two ratings, one for concert and another for sight reading. The ratings are Superior, Excellent, Good, Fair and Poor and there is no ranking of bands or selecting outstanding ensembles.

The Festival averages twelve bands with at least half the bands being from elementary or middle school/junior high schools. The bands are generally from within a 50 mile radius of East Stroudsburg.

The areas of preparation for hosting the Festival are: 1) securing judges; 2) a bulk mailing to area schools to encourage them to participate; and 3) establishing student committees that take care of the logistics on the day of the Festival.

The judges are selected with consideration given to their musicianship, their ability to communicate in a positive and constructive manner, and their reputation. They should live within 150 miles of East Stroudsburg to keep travel expenses at a minimum. It has proven most successful to have three judges for the concert performance with two who teach at the college or university level and one who teaches at the public school level. With this combination of judges, the comments and ratings have a good balance of opinions.

To publicize and encourage participation in the Festival, a bulk mailing is sent to all music teachers in the 80 neighboring school districts. An emphasis is placed upon elementary and junior high school participation since these students generally do not have conflicts with work schedules or sports activities and are available to travel with their band to the Festival.

The third area of preparation in hosting the Festival is the establishment of student committees that function on the day of the Festival. By using approximately 40 students, the Festival runs very smoothly. The committees are: registration table, judges' assistants, sight reading, stage crew, traffic, guides (two per band), ushers, announcer, and judges' luncheon.

Of course, the other area of consideration is to prepare the band for its participation in the Festival. The three selections are generally chosen from the N.B.A. Selected Music List in grade level six. However, the state allows that music may be performed that is not on the list and music that is either a recent publication or an "out-of-print" composition has been used. This flexibility allows the band to use music that will also adapt to the programming for the Spring Concert in May. The music is chosen for its challenge to the ensemble and for its contrast in styles: an orchestral transcription, a "traditional" band composition and a recent publication.

Spring Concert

The annual Spring Concert, held in mid May, is the culmination of the year's work. The three major considerations are: 1) selection of music; 2) engaging a guest soloist; and 3) preparing the 16 to 20 page program.

Usually included in the selection of music is a traditional transcription generally taken from the Romantic period of orchestral literature. These works of the Romantic composers are very compatible to the large Concert Band. Also these pieces, such as Moussorgsky's "Night on Bald Mountain," Rossini's "William Tell Overture" or Tchaikovsky's "1812 Overture," are available on numerous recordings which are excellent teaching aids and help to create the students' interest and appreciation for serious orchestral music.

Two or three selections are chosen from the ever-expanding literature of music written specifically for the concert band. These selections form an excellent contrast in musical style with the Romantic orchestral transcription. Usually they employ more percussion requirements, twentieth century harmonies and create a unique rehearsal problem. The problem being that the technical demands on the players are generally not as demanding for the young players as the orchestral works, but it is difficult for the young players to develop musical phrases out of twentieth century music.

Several senior band members will be featured as soloists. Senior soloists are very good for the program from the audience interest standpoint. However, in an effort to keep the number of solo selections to a minimum, trios or duets have been used. The other consideration very important for a satisfying performance is that the band must be well prepared with the accompaniment in order for the soloist to feel secure.

Keeping in mind that the majority of people in the audience are parents and friends and not musically trained individuals, the first half of the concert will be the more serious selections. After intermission the guest artist is featured and the concert concludes with a show tune or movie score and a Sousa March.

Due to the school's proximity to New York City and Philadelphia, the band has been able to have guest artists who are members of either the New York Philharmonic or the Philadelphia Orchestra. These musicians have been most encouraging, cooperative, appreciative and understanding in their collaboration with the band.

The direction of this guest artist program is to eventually have a soloist appear with the band on each of the band instruments. To date, soloists have. included: Paige Brooke, flute, New York Philharmonic; Frank Kaderabek, trumpet, Philadelphia Orchestra; Edward Erwin, trombone, New York Philharmonic; Raoul Querze, clarinet, Philadelphia Orchestra and Harvey Phillips, tuba, Indiana University.

After the soloist has been engaged, a rehearsal time must be established and music selected. Due to the soloist's commitments to his orchestra, scheduling for a rehearsal may be limited to the morning of the concert which has proven satisfactory. But in the case of the two New York Philharmonic soloists, they drove out during the week of the concert for an extra rehearsal. Selection of solo literature with band accompaniment can be a problem. There is a great deal of brass literature written for the bands of Arthur Pryor, Patrick Conway and John Philip Sousa. However, there is very limited literature available for the woodwind instruments. Sources of solo literature have come from suggestions by Leonard Smith, conductor of the Detroit Concert Band and the service bands in Washington, D.C. The librarians of the United States Marine Band and the United States Army Band have been extremely cooperative in suggesting solos and even in loaning arrangements that are not published.

If possible, the soloist will also play a trio or quartet with students from the band. The service bands have been invaluable in suggesting compositions of this nature.

In addition to performing a solo with the band, these musicians have taken time to talk to the band about their careers, the value and importance of music in the school, their approach to life, the need for systematic practice and an understanding that many of the students in the band will choose a career other than music but that the discipline of playing an instrument will serve them throughout their lives. Often the soloist speaks to the audience with his observations about the students or the music program in general. This personal touch is very impressive to the non-musicians in the audience.

An extensive 16 to 20 page 8 by 11 inch program is prepared for the concert. The concert program includes photographs of the seniors, photograph and biography of the guest artist, band personnel, the program, Seniors Look Back, acknowledgements, staff, Executive Committee and a chronological list of the band's activities and achievements for the year. Almost all this material is typed up and made photocopy ready. In this way, the cost of the program is reduced because the printer does not have to typeset these pages.

Another means of reducing the cost of the program

is to make a stencil and run off the two or three pages of program notes which are then inserted into the program. There have been three sources of information for program notes. Quite often, the conductor's score will include biographical information about the composer and a paragraph or two of program notes about the piece. The second source of information has been the Norman E. Smith and Albert Stoutamire book entitled "Band Music Notes." The third source is to contact the composer and/or the publisher. Although time consuming, the preparation of the program notes can be very educational for the students, audience and especially the director.

The financing of the program is covered by advertisements from the local merchants and patron listings. The ten to twelve pages of advertisements are collected by the officers of the band and the directors. It has been helpful to have copies of the previous year's program for the students to show prospective advertisers and to approach merchants who have previously advertised. The patron listings are supported primarily by the parents and the students themselves. The students have fun with their creative listings such as, "The Tranquillizing Trombone Quartet," "Super Saxes" and "The Double Trouble Tooter Flutes."

Prior to the final selection on the concert, several awards are presented and the senior members of the band are recognized. The awards include the Carrie H. Rogers Memorial Award, a $3000 scholarship for a student to pursue an education in music; the Band Booster Award; the American Federation of Musicians' $50 Award; the Band Parents $400 Scholarship; the John Philip Sousa Award; The Barbara Fatzinger Award which is given in memory of the former band director; and the Clement Wiedinmyer Award, a $300 scholarship which is given in memory of the band's first director.

The spring concert is the culmination of the year's work. A great deal of effort is put forth in the preparation of the approximately 90 minutes of music, the presentation of the guest soloist and the printed program. Through all this work, an emphasis is placed upon serious music performed as well as possible.

4 THE JUNIOR HIGH BAND PROGRAM

This chapter is by Patrick C. Dorian, Junior High Band Director, East Stroudsburg Area School District.

The East Stroudsburg Junior High instrumental program involves approximately 80 seventh and eighth grade students. Although almost all of these students have been in an instrumental program since fourth grade, interested students are welcome to begin playing an instrument in junior high. Various styles of music ranging from classical to popular are performed in the concert band. Band members are expected to participate in all concert and marching activities including lessons, rehearsals, and performances.

Instrumentation

In a concert band of 80 students I consider the following to be a balanced instrumentation: 4 first flutes, 8 second flutes, 2 oboes, 2 bassoons, 4 first clarinets, 8 second clarinets, 10 third clarinets, 2 alto clarinets, 2 bass clarinets, 2 first alto saxophones, 4 second alto saxophones, 2 tenor saxophones, 1 baritone saxophone, 3 first trumpets, 4 second trumpets, 4 third trumpets, 4 horns, 4 trombones, 2 euphoniums, 1 tuba, and 7 percussion players. Of course this instrumentation cannot always be exact and some variance in these numbers is not a problem. However, close communication with the elementary instrumental director (fourth through sixth grades) helps to feed a balanced instrumentation into the junior high each year.

As can be noted above, more players are selected for second and third parts than for first parts. Since melody is more easily heard, having more second and third players helps fill out the harmony to achieve a balanced sound. Also, the range and technical demands of first parts can be handled only by the best players, which usually amounts to a rather small percentage of each section. Most of my junior high students have just come from the elementary music program where they performed Grade 2 music and are challenged by the Grade 4 music (National Band Association grading system) performed by the junior high band. Giving these students second and third parts makes their transition from elementary to junior high band a positive one. They are playing parts that are demanding but usually not too difficult for them.

Scheduling

The junior high band rehearses 35 minutes during the school day three times a week. Each student is also scheduled for a 40 minute weekly lesson during school time with his/her section. The lesson schedule is rotated carefully so that a student will only miss a particular class an average of three times per nine-week marking period. This lesson rotation is also planned on a day rotating schedule, making it possible for a student not to miss a particular class on the same day as he/she had for a previous lesson. Therefore, if a teacher plans a review every Thursday, it may affect a band student only once per nine-week marking period. (Students stay in class when tests are given.) If a student feels uncomfortable missing a certain class, arrangements can be made for the lesson to be made up after school or during a free period. Since no lessons are scheduled on Fridays, make-up lessons can be given then.

A four-week summer program from the last week of July to the third week in August is offered to all interested students. There is no cost to the students for this program. Each student participating in the summer program is scheduled for a 40-minute lesson once a week with his/her section and two 90-minute band rehearsals per week. The amount of students participating in the four-week program fluctuates due to summer vacations, jobs, and so forth; in spite of this fluctuation, the program is effective in that it provides an opportunity for students to play, encouraging them to practice throughout the summer. What they have been taught during the school year is reinforced and any further progress is a bonus.

Music Selection

An attempt is made to play as many different styles of music as possible including transcriptions from the baroque, classical, and romantic periods; contemporary concert works; movie or show medleys; pop tunes; and marches. I prefer to stay within the Grade 4 level since the students are able to play this level of music well after working hard—they are challenged but not frustrated by the difficulty of the music. Since the high school performs Grade 6 music, the students are prepared to graduate to this level after two years in the junior high band.

In selecting music for a concert performance two marches are chosen. One of these marches is in $\frac{6}{8}$ meter and the other is in $\frac{2}{4}$, $\frac{4}{4}$, or cut-time. The march in $\frac{2}{4}$, $\frac{4}{4}$, or cut-time is usually handed out early in the fall. In October the students are given Ray Shahin's arrangement of the Thanksgiving song "Over the River" in $\frac{6}{8}$ meter. Most members of the band are familiar with this well-known holiday song. A $\frac{6}{8}$ rhythm pattern sheet is also distributed and $\frac{6}{8}$ meter is then taught at a slow tempo (6 beats to the measure). Over a ten-day period I gradually accelerate the tempo until the students play it at 120 pulses per minute with foot taps on eighth-note counts one and four of each measure. The band performs "Over the River" in a November concert and is then well prepared to start working on a $\frac{6}{8}$ march.

Since the junior high band marches in several parades each year during May and June, the two marches also can be played in the parades. In band rehearsal, to prepare the students for marching, they are taught to lightly tap their left foot (with their heel remaining on the floor) on the first pulse of each measure and their right foot on the second pulse of each measure. This helps the students to learn to stay in step when they eventually march. Both marches are played at 120 pulses per minute and the students learn to subdivide the pulse into three parts in the $\frac{6}{8}$ march and two parts in the $\frac{2}{4}$, $\frac{4}{4}$, or cut-time march. See Figure 8.

Studio PR/Columbia publishes a series of eight simplified marches by Mike Story; these marches are "block scored" for the fullest possible sound and are good for junior high students learning to play and march at the same time.

Almost every year a composer is commissioned to write a piece for the junior high band. Before the composer

Note: Foot tapping of alternate feet is used only with pieces that the students will eventually march to. On all other selections only one foot is tapped with the pulse.

Figure 8

begins, I discuss instrumentation and student abilities with him/her. We agree on a deadline so that the students have their parts for a reasonable amount of time before the premier of the piece. If possible, the composer conducts the students at the premier performance. Past commissioned composers have included Elliott Del Borgo, Jerry Nowak, and Sy Brandon.

Rehearsal

Time is used as efficiently as possible in the 35-minute rehearsal period that we have three times per week. When the students enter the band room they are told to carefully take out their instruments and to sit down immediately (socialize later!). If time permits for what I have planned on a particular day, I sell reeds, unstick mouthpieces, make minor instrument repairs, and hand out music. During this time the students should be adjusting their stands, chairs, neck straps, and tuning slides.

The rehearsal begins with announcements of future events and details on how we will prepare for these events. I also announce which students have lessons the following day and then give the order of the two or three pieces we are about to rehearse. The students are then reminded to sit up straight with their feet flat on the floor, to think "up and out," and to stretch their "spines to the sky." These rules are from the **Alexander Technique**, which is a study of the most efficient way to position the body.

We start as a group by playing the **Warm Up—Tune Up—Tone Up** exercises that John Paynter used when I was a graduate student at Northwestern University. These exercises are performed very rubato while covering the band's complete dynamic range. The students are trained from the beginning of the rehearsal to watch the conductor and to listen carefully to the blend of the entire band.

From September to mid-November the band prepares for the pre-Thanksgiving concert. December to May is spent rehearsing for an adjudication festival and spring concert. Mid-May to June is spent preparing for parades. I find it is easier to teach the students basic marching indoors before rehearsing outside.

Lessons

After students assemble their instruments I ask for their *Daily Practice Record* (see Figures 9 and 10), which must be signed by one or both of their parents *after* the sheet is filled in. If the record sheet is not signed the student has one week to have it completed. These sheets are returned to the students after they have been graded—the grades are determined by how much practice time has been completed and how well a student does in his/her lessons. When a practice record is turned in, a new one is then issued to the student after I fill in the student's name and the starting day (in the Practice Time column) that begins a new week of practice.

Each group lesson starts with long tones to develop the student's natural embouchure—I let the students place their mouthpieces where they feel most comfortable unless their embouchure is off center a great deal. I use Carmine Caruso's "long setting" method from his **Musical Calisthenics for Brass** (published by Columbia Pictures Publications). Although some teachers feel that Caruso's techniques are unorthodox, after studying with him for eight years I believe his ideas expand range, improve air flow, increase tonal vitality, and increase dynamic range quickly and efficiently.

Next the students take out their scale sheets and we cover the chromatic scale and one major scale that I choose. Each student has a scale sheet containing the

Name ....

EAST STROUDSBURG BANDS
DAILY PRACTICE RECORD

LESSON GRADE ....

The importance of DAILY practice cannot be overemphasized if a student is to make satisfactory progress on his/her instrument. Students should be on a consistent program of daily practice sessions.

Students should choose a definite time to practice each and every day in a well-lit, quiet room away from the distractions of friends, brothers and sisters, television, and the stereo.

Students are expected to practice a minimum of thirty minutes EVERY DAY.

Parental cooperation is requested by their signature(s) at the end of the week.

ASSIGNMENT	**PRACTICE TIME**
CHROMATIC SCALE;	SUN. .../... .... Min.
MAJOR SCALES, ESPE-	MON. .../... .... Min.
CIALLY THE	TUE. .../... .... Min.
SCALE;	WED. .../... .... Min.
CURRENT BAND MUSIC;	THUR.. .../... .... Min.
PAGE NO. ..... IN YOUR	FRI. .../... .... Min.
LESSON BOOK.	SAT. .../... .... Min.
	TOTAL .... Min.

Parent's Signature (s) ....

....

(continued)

Figure 9

ADDITIONAL PRACTICE DAYS:

EXAMPLE:
SUNDAY   12/7   60 Min.

SUNDAY	. . . . . . /	. . . . Min.
MONDAY	. . . . . . /	. . . . Min.
TUESDAY	. . . . . . /	. . . . Min.
WEDNESDAY	. . . . . . /	. . . . Min.
THURSDAY	. . . . . . /	. . . . Min.
FRIDAY	. . . . . . /	. . . . Min.
SATURDAY	. . . . . . /	. . . . Min.
SUNDAY	. . . . . . /	. . . . Min.
MONDAY	. . . . . . /	. . . . Min.
TUESDAY	. . . . . . /	. . . . Min.
WEDNESDAY	. . . . . . /	. . . . Min.
THURSDAY	. . . . . . /	. . . . Min.
FRIDAY	. . . . . . /	. . . . Min.
SATURDAY	. . . . . . /	. . . . Min.

Figure 10

chromatic scale and all major scales written out for the entire range of their instrument. When playing music I want each student to know the names of the notes they are playing, so for the chromatic scale I have one student name all of the ascending notes and another student name all of the descending notes. After playing the chromatic scale, we go on to the major scale I have chosen. I select a student to name how many flats or sharps are in the key signature. A student then names the accidentals in the key signature in order from left to right. Next someone names the pitches of the scale for one octave. I then ask if there are any questions about fingerings, and the group plays the scale ascending and descending for one or two octaves depending on what they are capable of. Corrections are made if necessary and the scale is always repeated for reinforcement.

Sometimes additional rhythm sheets are made up using characteristic rhythms from our current band music. The more complex rhythms are written in rhythmic values that are double the length of the original rhythms, thus simplifying the rhythms so the students can practice them and gradually increase speed. These rhythms are played on a single pitch with steady foot tapping.

Example:
The rhythm as it appears in the piece:

On rhythm sheet it could also be written as:

Next we work on our more challenging band pieces and if time permits we play an easier piece that the students choose from their band folders. Frequently I demonstrate various musical concepts on my trumpet or I sing an excerpt we are working on at correct pitch. I believe strongly in teachers as performers since the best way to teach something is often to demonstrate it. Demonstrations make lessons more interesting and give students a break from playing which is sometimes needed. I think it is also important for students to sing excerpts and clap rhythms because problem passages then can be isolated without playing. The student does not have to worry about blowing, articulation, fingering, key signature (when clapping), and dynamics.

Percussion lessons are run in the same format as wind lessons with rudiments and rolls used instead of scales.

Grading

Students grades are determined by the following.
1. number of lessons attended
2. grades from **Daily Practice Records** submitted and number of records submitted
3. behavior and contribution in lessons and band rehearsal
4. audition results (second marking period only)
5. extra credit performances in small ensembles, jazz ensembles, churches, and community events

A major part of the second marking period grade is the seating audition (see Figures 11 and 12). This audition is comparable to a large exam in another class, and is

WIND INSTRUMENTS AUDITION FORM
EAST STROUDSBURG
JUNIOR HIGH SCHOOL BAND

NAME______________________________DATE_____________

INSTRUMENT________________________

SCALES:

    Chromatic - (20)

    Major - (15 each)

C   D♭   D   E♭   F   G♭   G   A♭   A   B♭   B

PREPARED PIECE:

    Tone (20)   ___________

    Articulation (15)   ___________

    Technique (15)   ___________

    Phrasing (15)   ___________

    Rhythm (15)   ___________

    Dynamics (15)   ___________

    Intonation (15)   ___________

    Interpretation (15)   ___________

    Foot Tap (15)   ___________

SIGHT-READING: (20)   ___________

                 TOTAL: _____________________

                 (Out Of A Possible 360)

COMMENTS:

Figure 11

PERCUSSION AUDITION FORM
EAST STROUDSBURG
JUNIOR HIGH SCHOOL BAND

NAME_________________________________ DATE ____________

RUDIMENTS AND ROLLS:

Long Roll (Open) (15) __________

	SLOW	MEDIUM	FAST
Paradiddle (5 Each)	_____	_____	_____
5 Stroke Roll (5 Each)	_____	_____	_____
7 Stroke Roll (5 Each)	_____	_____	_____
9 Stroke Roll (5 Each)	_____	_____	_____
11 Stroke Roll (5 Each)	_____	_____	_____
13 Stroke Roll (5 Each)	_____	_____	_____
15 Stroke Roll (5 Each)	_____	_____	_____
17 Stroke Roll (5 Each)	_____	_____	_____

SOLO:

Rhythm (15) __________

Dynamics (15) __________

Technique (15) __________

Foot Tap (15) __________

SIGHT-READING: (20) __________

TOTAL: ____________________

(Out Of A Possible 215)

COMMENTS:

Figure 12

done during the second and third weeks of December. All students must be auditioned before the December break so that the band can be seated the first day that school is back in session in January. (From September to December seating is arranged with the eighth graders on the first parts.)

Preparation for the audition procedure starts in mid-October. Eighth graders usually need less preparation than seventh graders since they are already accustomed to auditioning. The audition begins with the chromatic scale (ascending and descending), which is worth twenty points. The students must play at least one octave at a medium tempo and they get more points (which can add up to twenty points) for playing more of the entire range of their instruments. More points are also given for speed as long as clarity and evenness are maintained. For example, if a student reads the chromatic scale for one octave at a slow speed he/she might receive eight points, whereas a student playing the scale from memory for the entire range of the instrument at a brisk tempo might be awarded nineteen points. Next to the number of points received an M or R is written to indicate whether the scale was played from memory or read.

Next the student names a major scale and plays it in the following rhythm pattern.

This rhythm pattern is also used in the high school and district band audition process. On the student's point sheet I indicate M or R and the number of complete octaves played. Speed, evenness, and clarity are taken into consideration in the scoring. Points are awarded for as many scales as are played. The term "awarded" is an important one because I want the students to feel that each scale learned is an accomplishment. I put a great deal of emphasis on scales throughout the junior band program.

The audition procedure also includes the playing of a prepared piece, which is usually one of the major concert pieces that the band will be working on in January. All of the players of a particular instrument receive the same part to prepare so the procedure is consistent. For example, all trumpeters prepare the first trumpet part. The music is distributed during late November and only three or four band rehearsals are used to explain the piece. No additional help is offered, encouraging the students to work on the music with each other or by themselves. By doing this, I can judge how ambitious the students are.

The final audition requirement is sight reading. All players of a particular instrument play the same sight-reading excerpt. Students are given two minutes to analyze the key signature and rhythms while they "finger" through the excerpt.

All auditions are private—only the student and myself are in the auditioning room. After the audition sheets are tabulated the students are seated in order by the highest score to the lowest score. If a student wants to move up in his/her section, the student applies to challenge the person in front of him/her. When the challenge forms are made available on February 1 (see Figure 13) the challenge procedures begin whenever necessary. Challenges are similar to auditions except that the "challenger" and "challengee" are behind a curtain (at different times) so I do not know which of the two students is playing.

EAST STROUDSBURG
JUNIOR BAND
CHALLENGE FORM

I, ______________________________ WISH

TO CHALLENGE ____________________________

TODAY'S DATE __________ / __________ / __________

DATE AND TIME OF CHALLENGE TO BE
SET BY MR. DORIAN

Figure 13

Performances

The junior high band performances for the year are as follows:

1. summer festival (mid-August) comprised of students involved in the summer program
2. combined half-time show with the high school marching show band and the elementary band (show takes place every other year in mid-October)
3. Halloween festival (if our schedule permits)
4. Sit-Down Revue (with the high school marching show band in November)
5. department concert (mid-March) with high school and elementary concert bands
6. concert band adjudication festival (April)
7. spring concert (May)
8. Memorial Day parade
9. firemen's parade (late June)

All performances except the summer festival are done in our junior band uniform, which consists of the following:

1. clean white shoes
2. clean white socks
3. clean white dress pants
4. long-sleeve white turtleneck (fall and winter) or short-sleeve white shirt (spring)
5. purple blazer with junior band insignia (supplied by school)

Objectives

The objectives for the junior high instrumental program are as follows:

1. to develop and maintain proper hand position, posture, inhalation, exhalation, and characteristic tone qualities for each individual instrument
2. to develop eye-hand-ear coordination; to learn the different mathematical subdivisions of the pulse
3. to develop basic aesthetic sensitivity
4. to maintain what is established at the elementary instrumental level, and to advance
5. to help each student find the most relaxed and efficient method of playing his/her instrument
6. to establish good habits in reading music, sight reading, reading ahead, recognizing articulations, note values, dynamics, and pitches; to interpret what is on the page cleanly and accurately
7. to help students recognize the value of maintaining and caring for their instruments
8. to establish the basic fundamentals of playing in tune
9. to begin to learn the different styles of the historical periods in music
10. to learn to play together in an ensemble in which the tempo is not always strict; to learn to follow the conductor; to develop confidence through performance
11. to develop pride in the students as individuals and as a group
12. to develop each student's character to his/her fullest potential through a sense of responsibility to the band program

I find the position of junior high instrumental director to be a challenging one since fifty percent of my students each year are new members to the band. Within a two-year period I must take them from the elementary band and prepare them for the high school band. At the junior high level, coordination tends to be undeveloped and peer pressure is often a problem. Persistence, patience, and understanding are necessary to correctly channel a great deal of energy; if this is done, the end results can be impressive.

5 OTHER ASPECTS OF THE BAND PROGRAM

Summer Band

The School District offers its instrumental music students a four-week program of group lessons and band rehearsals during the last week in July and the first three weeks in August. All students in grades four through twelve are invited to participate in the program and approximately 80% of the students take advantage of the program.

The students are divided into four groups for their instruction: beginners, elementary band, junior band, and senior band. The instruction is given by the school's three teachers with assistance by senior high students. All of the instruction is done in the high school building which develops a role model of the older students for the younger students.

The elementary students (grades 4 through 6) are divided into two groups. One group, the beginners, who are receiving their first instruction on their instrument, have two lessons a week and a band rehearsal. The teacher is generally assisted by a high school student in the lessons since the classes are homogeneously grouped with as many as 12 students in a class.

The other group of elementary students are the children who are already playing an instrument. These students receive a group lesson and four band rehearsals per week. Again, assistance in the instruction is given by high school students which helps to develop the role model of the older student.

The junior high students (grades 7 and 8) receive a group lesson and two band rehearsals per week. For the incoming seventh graders, this is their first experience in the junior high band. It also gives the eighth graders a sense of importance as they will now be the older students in the junior high band. Again, senior high students assist with the instruction.

The senior high students (grades 9 through 12) recieve a group lesson and two band rehearsals per week. The lessons and one of the band rehearsals are given during the time schedule of 9:00 A.M. to 1:00 P.M. However, the other band rehearsal is held in the evening. This scheduling is done to accommodate student work commitments.

At the conclusion of the four-week summer program, the four bands join with the Band Parents organization to present their Summer Festival. The Festival is an evening of music, games and food. Each of the four bands perform, starting with the beginner's band at 6:30 P.M. and followed by the Elementary Band, the Junior High Band at 7:30 P.M., and the High School Band at 8:30 P.M. In addition to the various band performances the Band Parents have booths and games of chance such as: baseball toss, football toss, shaving cream throws, lollipop tree, white elephant table, duck pond, sand box, hay ride, hot dogs, soda, pop corn, ice cream, cotton candy and a corn roast. Also, the traditional "cake walk" which is a variation on musical chairs. For 20¢, one can join the circle of people competing to win one of the cakes, which have been donated by the parents. The people in the circle walk as long as the band plays. When the music stops an arrow is spun and when it comes to rest, the person it points to wins the cake. This event is most enjoyable to all participants, the band, and the spectators. The total profit from the Festival has averaged about $2,000 and is an evening of family participation with the students supplying the music and the parents taking care of the other activities.

Facilities, Inventory, and Budget

As previously noted, the Elementary Band rehearses at the elementary school located in town. However, the elementary band director travels to the students' home school for students to receive their weekly lesson.

The Junior and Senior High Bands, including the Jazz Ensemble, rehearse in the high school bandroom. In addition to the bandroom (45' x 60'), there are two offices, one each for the Director of Bands and his Associate and four practice rooms. The bandroom area is conveniently located across the hall from the 1,000 seat auditorium. Additional space is required for 1) the storage of the music library which is very extensive, including band music, solo music and chamber music; 2) uniform storage; and 3) instrument storage.

The school owns an extensive inventory of instruments. For the marching band, the school supplies piccolos for all the flute players (16), alto saxophones for clarinet players who double, tenor saxophones, mellophoniums for the French horn players, large bore trombones, brass sousaphones, percussion equipment, plus band front equipment of rifles and flags. The uniform is the traditional style with jacket, trousers, overlay, Pershing style hat. Students are also issued a heavy duty rain coat and garment bag. For the Concert Band, the school supplies the following instruments: piccolo, English horn, oboes, bassoons, alto, bass and contrabass clarinets, soprano, tenor and baritone saxophones, double French horns, flugel horn, bass trombone, four value euphoniums, four value tubas, and double bass. Since the Concert Band wears the traditional black concert attire, the boys are issued a tuxedo. For the Jazz Ensemble, the school supplies soprano, tenor and baritone saxophones, flugel horn, bass trombone, electric piano, double bass, electric bass and drum set.

The financing of the Elementary and Junior high bands is covered entirely by the school district. However, the funding of the high school band comes from two sources — the school district and the Band Parents Organization.

The school district funding of the high school band covers instruments, uniforms, music, basic supplies, District, Regional and All State Band and Orchestra registration fees, clinician's fees, and the salary for a part-time secretary.

The Band Parents funding helps to defray the cost of the extra-curricular activities such as band camps (marching and concert), trips, band banquet, Spring Concert flowers, and a picnic.

Band Parents Organization

The Band Parents organization is open to all parents of Junior and Senior High band members. They have been active since 1939 and presently have a $10,000 to $12,000 annual budget. They meet the second Monday of the month in the bandroom. The format of the meeting includes old business, new business, director's report of activities that took place during the past month and upcoming events. The meeting may be concluded with a brief student performance or demonstration.

For a typical Band Parents budget, see Figure 14.

District/Regional/All-State Bands and Orchestras

Pennsylvania is divided into 12 geographical Districts which feed six Regions and finally the All-State ensembles. In order to participate in an All-State ensemble, a student must first be successful at District and Regional auditions.

Each member of the high school band is given the District Band audition piece during the summer. (This solo is also used for the seating audtions of the Concert Band held in January.) The District Band audition also includes nine required scales, chromatic scale and sight reading.

Prior to the December District Band audition, the director will work with each auditioning student three times. The first session, in October, is to give the student a general direction for practice, to correct any wrong notes or incorrect rhythms and to clarify the scale requirements. The second session is to check for a consistent tone throughout the range of the scales, set the tempo for the scales, set the tempo of the solo and work on the phrasing and style of interpretation. The third session is to simulate the actual audition procedure and atmosphere. These sessions are held either after school or in the evening, thus accomodating the students who either work or have after school practices for an athletic team or club meetings.

EAST STROUDSBURG BAND PARENTS BUDGET

DISBURSEMENTS

Fall Trip	$ 3,000.00
Banquet	1,500.00
Concert Band Camp	1,000.00
Jazz Trip	1,000.00
Picnic	50.00
Summer Band Camp	3,400.00
Scholarship	400.00
Advertising	200.00
Miscellaneous	200.00
Total	$10,400.00

INCOME

Summer Festival	$ 2,000.00
Community Calendar	300.00
Stadium Cushions	200.00
Hoagie Sales (2)	4,000.00
Ski Swap	750.00
Bake Sales (2)	400.00
Hot Dog Sales (2)	200.00
Easter Candy	800.00
Tag Day	950.00
Auction	200.00
IGA Tapes	500.00
Interest	100.00
Total	$10,400.00

Figure 14

Students are encouraged to audition for District Band with the emphasis upon the positive aspects of auditioning. Although not all students are accepted, each student becomes a better musician due to the extra practice, extra instruction and the audition. Approximately 35 students audition with 12 students being accepted.

The selected students receive their music the day of the audition and then have about a month or more to prepare for the three-day District Festival. At the Festival, the students are reauditioned for seating and the students in the top chairs will combine with students from another District Band to form one of the 6 Regional Bands in the state. Reauditions are also held at the 3-day Regional Festival with the top students going on to the All-State Band.

In order to prepare the students for these reauditions, the director will rehearse the students together three or four times and, if available, play recordings of the music being prepared.

Communications/Public Relations

A newsletter is prepared three or four times a year. It presents, chronologically, the band's various activities and programs. The newsletter is generally six type-written pages and is sent via bulk mail to the parents of the Junior and Senior High Band members, administrators, Board of Education members, area band directors and friends of the band. It has been reproduced and used in several college method classes as an example of what is possible in a public school music program.

The other avenue available for public relations is the local paper with press releases about concerts, invitational performances, guest artists and District, Regional and All State participants.

WHY HAVE A JAZZ ENSEMBLE PROGRAM
by Patrick C. Dorian

As the jazz ensemble director of one junior high jazz ensemble and two high school jazz ensembles, I am able to involve 55 students in the study and appreciation of a musical form that originated and developed in America. With a jazz ensemble program in addition to a concert band program, we offer students the opportunity to receive a well-rounded musical education.

While a jazz ensemble may involve a group of twenty students, it also demands independence of each student since there is only one player on a part. If a part is not played well the quality of the ensemble suffers. Jazz requires as much discipline as any other musical form because players must concern themselves with intonation, style, dynamics, tone, and playing as a unit. The technical and range demands as well as the harmonic complexities of jazz strengthen performers' abilities to play other types of music.

Jazz improvisation is a creative process that develops ear-to-hand coordination and gets the player away from the printed page. Although not all students will excel in improvisational skills, the highly advanced techniques they are studying will contribute to making them better players. Each of my high school students is required to write out chords, practice them, and play them for me. I feel that true proficiency of a concept is accomplished *after* the student obtains the knowledge *and* the skills, not one or the other.

JAZZ ENSEMBLE PERFORMANCES

Second week in December: Advanced high school jazz ensemble performs at the Christmas dinner/dance for the local Rotary club (30-minute listening set and 60-minute dance set).

Third week in December: Both high school jazz ensembles perform jazz Christmas selections at the District Holiday Choral Concert.

Last day of school before winter break: Both high school jazz ensembles perform a Christmas assembly with the high school choir.

Late January/early February: The junior high and senior high jazz ensembles perform accompaniment selections while members of the band front do routines in the Jazz Ensemble/Band Front Revue.

First weekend in March: The junior high jazz ensemble performs at a junior high jazz ensemble adjudication festival.

Late March: Both high school jazz ensembles perform at a college or university jazz festival such as Berklee School of Music or University of New Hampshire. This is a weekend trip for the students.

Late April: The junior and senior high jazz ensembles perform their spring concert with the junior and high school show choirs. A well-known soloist performs with the jazz ensembles. Past soloists have included Phil Woods, Urbie Green, Marvin Stamm, Lou Marini, Jr., and Al Cohn.

The ensembles are available as much as possible for community events such as telethons and benefit dances.

6   A BAND DIRECTOR'S SCHEDULE OF "THINGS TO DO"

July and August

1.) Design and chart halftime show

2.) Contact a guest composer/conductor for March's Instrumental Music Department Concert

3.) Private teaching to help the more advanced students

4.) Summer Band Program (four weeks of lessons and band rehearsals)

5.) Five day band camp

6.) Band Parents' outdoor Summer Festival with the Beginning, Elementary, Junior and Senior High Bands performing

7.) Uniform distribution

8.) Confirm accomodations at a motel for the Marching Show Band's Fall trip

9.) Contract chartered bus company for the Fall trip

September and October

1.) Band Parents Meeting the second Monday of each month

2.) Performances at football games every weekend

3.) Performances at two local cavalcades

4.) Hoagie (submarine sandwich) Sale

5.) Senior bandmembers select music and chart a halftime show

6.) Halloween Parade

7.) Students sign up to audition for District Band and Orchestra (work with each student at least three times prior to the December audition)

8.) Contact three judges for April's Concert Band Adjudication Festival

9.) Contact guest soloist for May's Spring Concert

10.) Contact a college (within a 50-mile radius) for January's Concert Band Camp

11.) Three-day trip with the Marching Show Band to include a performance at a professional football game and sight seeing

November and December

1.) Band Parents Meeting the second Monday of each month

2.) Performances of Seniors' halftime show with recognition of their parents on the field

3.) Marching "Sit Down" Revue and Band Parents' Bake Sale featuring the music and band front routines of the marching season

4.) Select music for February's Jazz Ensemble/Band Front Revue

5.) Football games conclude with the Thanksgiving Day Game

6.) Band Banquet

7.) Continue to work individually with students auditioning for District Band and Orchestra

8.) Bulk mailing to all band directors within a seventy mile radius publicizing April's Concert Band Adjudication Festival

9.) Contact guest soloist for April's Jazz Ensemble concert

10.) Jazz Ensemble performs at Rotary Club's Dinner Dance

11.) Jazz Ensemble performs on Chorale Christmas concert

12.) Confirm motel accomodations for January's Concert Band Camp

13.) Bulk mailing of a Band Newsletter with a review of the year's activities to date

14.) District Band and Orchestra auditions

January and February

1.) Band Parents Meeting the second Monday of each month

2.) Concert Band auditions

3.) Contact professional football teams about a performance for next Fall

4.) Hoagie (submarine sandwich) Sale

5.) Concert Band Camp

6.) District Band and Orchestra Festivals

7.) Jazz Ensemble/Band Front Revue

8.) Confirm music selection with guest soloist for May's Spring Concert

9.) Jazz Ensembles perform on local television station's telethon

10.) Submit budget to building principal

March and April

1.) Band Parents Meeting the second Monday of each month

2.) Instrumental Music Department Concert (Elementary, Junior and Senior High Bands) with guest composer/conductor

3.) Jazz Ensembles three-day trip to perform at a Jazz Festival

4.) Saint Patrick's Day Parade

5.) Junior High Jazz Ensemble performs at a local Jazz Festival

6.) Continue to correspond with professional football teams to confirm performance date for next Fall

7.) Host Concert Band Adjudication Festival

8.) Jazz Ensemble/Swing Choir Concert with guest soloist

9.) Regional Band and Orchestra Festivals

10.) Nominate two students for the McDonald's All-American Band

11.) Contract a facility for August's Band Camp

12.) Organize students to solicit ads for the Spring Concert program

May and June

1.) Band Parents Meetings conclude with the May meeting and election of officers for the next year

2.) State music convention with All State ensembles performing

3.) Junior High Band/Chorus Concert

4.) Junior High Band/Chorus trip to local amusement park

5.) Spring Concert with guest soloist

6.) Memorial Day Parade

7.) Select music for first halftime show for next year

8.) Band Front tryouts for next year's squads

9.) Tryouts for third grade students with their parents who will be starting an instrument during the four-week summer band program

10.) Uniform collection

11.) Graduation Ceremony

12.) Contact parents and former students for chaperoning of August's Band Camp

13.) Assist students to prepare an audition tape for the McDonald's All-American Band

14.) Meet with new Band Parents officers to prepare a budget for the next school year

ABOUT THE AUTHORS

Gordon Fung earned his undergraduate degree from Ithaca College and received his Master's Degree from Southern Illinois University. He has studied horn with Joseph Singer of the New York Philharmonic and Herbert Pierson of the Philadelphia Orchestra.

Mr. Fung has taught in New York, Illinois, and is presently Director of Bands for the East Stroudsburg, Pennsylvania Area School District. Under his direction the East Stroudsburg High School Concert Band has given several premiere performances including commissioned works by Elliot Del Borgo and Harry Simeone; received numerous "superior" ratings; and has established a $35,000 endowment fund for music scholarships for its graduates. The East Stroudsburg High School Marching-Show Band has also received numerous "superior" ratings and performs annually for both Canadian and National Football League teams.

Mr. Fung has served as a member of the Pennsylvania Music Educators Association Executive Council, State Chairman for P.M.E.A. Adjudication Festivals, Pennsylvania State Chairman for the National Band Association and is presently on the N.B.A. Board of Directors. He has guest conducted and adjudicated throughout the Northeast and has had articles published in "The Instrumentalist" and the state journals of New York, New Jersey and Pennsylvania.

Mr. Fung is a member of the International Horn Society, P.M.E.A., M.E.N.C., N.B.A., Pi Kappa Lambda, and Phi Beta Mu. He was selected the 1983 "Educator of the Year" by the local Rotary Club, and has been the recipient of both the P.M.E.A. "Citation of Excellence" and the N.B.A. "Citation of Excellence."

Patrick C. Dorian holds the B.M. in Music Education and Music Performance from Ithaca College and the M.M. in Music Performance from Northwestern University. He has done postgraduate work at the Eastman School of Music and Pennsylvania State University. Since 1980 Dorian has been Director of Jazz Ensembles and Associate Director of Bands in the East Stroudsburg, Pennsylvania Area School District.

His junior high concert band has received several superior ratings at Adjudication Festivals sponsored by the Pennsylvania Music Educators Association and has premiered compositions by such composers as Elliot Del Borgo and Jerry Nowak. He is the 1983 recipient of the National Band Association's Outstanding Jazz Educator Award. Mr. Dorian's jazz ensembles have performed with such guest soloists as Phil Woods, Urbie Green, Marvin Stamm, Al Cohn, Bob Dorough, George Young, Kim Parker, and Bill Dobbins.

Mr. Dorian's upper-level jazz ensemble was named "Outstanding Jazz Ensemble" at the 1983 Mansfield State University Jazz Festival, placed second at the 1984 Berklee School of Music Jazz festival, and was named "Outstanding Jazz Ensemble" at the 1985 University of New Hampshire Jazz Festival.

Mr. Dorian has adjudicated at jazz and marching band festivals in the Mid-Atlantic area and has been a guest lecturer/clinician/adjudicator at Mansfield State University. He is also a teacher-artist of jazz studies at Moravian College. His articles have been published in "The Instrumentalist" and the "P.M.E.A. News." He is active in the National Association of Jazz Educators, the National Band Association, M.E.N.C., P.M.E.A., the International Trumpet Guild, Pi Kappa Lambda, the College Music Society, and the American Federation of Musicians.

ACKNOWLEDGEMENTS

Typesetting: Jane Masich, The P.A. Hutchison Co.

Cover: Reggi Henning

Printing: The P.A. Hutchison Co.